EDWIN MORGAN TWENTIES

SCOTLAND

CELEBRATING EDWIN MORGAN'S CENTENARY

Love
Scotland
Menagerie
Take Heart
Space and Spaces

EDWIN MORGAN TWENTIES

SCOTLAND

SELECTED POEMS

Introduced by
Liz Lochhead

Polygon

in association with
Carcanet

First published in Great Britain in 2020 by
Polygon, an imprint of Birlinn Ltd, in association with
Carcanet Press Ltd

Birlinn Ltd
West Newington House
10 Newington Road
Edinburgh EH9 1QS

9 8 7 6 5 4 3 2 1

www.polygonbooks.co.uk

ISBN 978 1 84697 544 8

British Library Cataloguing-in-Publication Data
A catalogue record for this book is available
from the British Library.

The publisher gratefully acknowledges investment from
Creative Scotland towards the publication of this book.

Typeset in Verdigris M V B by Polygon, Edinburgh
Printed and bound by Gutenberg, Malta

CONTENTS

INTRODUCTION

There is a famous 1980 painting by Sandy Moffat called *Poets' Pub*. This composite portrait, set in an amalgam of a few favourite Edinburgh haunts and howffs, came from separate preparatory studies made of the major Scottish poets in the late 1970s. Ranged around the central figure of Hugh MacDiarmid holding court are Norman MacCaig, Sorley MacLean, Iain Crichton Smith, George Mackay Brown, Sydney Goodsir Smith, Robert Garioch, Alan Bold and Edwin Morgan.

In reality, though, I can't see Morgan fitting in to this gathering – not the pubbable or clubbable type. While on friendly terms with all of these near-contemporaries, after sharing a platform at a public reading he'd much more likely have been on the second-last train home to Glasgow than wreathed in argument, feuds and flytings, nips of whisky and a masculine fug of tweedy pipe smoke in the Abbotsford, Milne's Bar or the Café Royal. In this painting Morgan isn't part of the central group but off to the side, his gaze looking outward, elsewhere.

As a Scottish poet, eccentric – but major.

The title of one of his best collections, *From Glasgow to Saturn*, just about delineates the range of his subject matter. At odds with the values of – although, as an only son, dutifully bound to – his douce, conservative, Protestant, prosperous parents, in his early poetry he struggled towards the freedom and release he found, when at the age of forty in 1960 he moved out to the other side of the city and came into his own, both falling in love and finding his voice, which was many voices. *A Second Life* (1968) proved him a virtuoso of nearly every form going. Almost to the very end of his long life he'd write everything from free verse to sonnets, concrete poems, sound poems, demotic dialogues, dramatic monologues – sometimes in the voice of the non-human something that did not have a voice till his listening imagination found it. Morgan was a shape-shifter and a time-traveller. He translated *Beowulf*. He was modernist, European, experimental always. Yet he credits the Beats and other American poets of the middle of last century with granting him the exhilarating permission that *poetry could be about anything*.

The poems in this quirky, provocative, always delightful selection are 'about' Scotland though. Part of a series (others are on love, animals, people, space) of five slim volumes, each containing twenty poems, making, in all, one hundred celebrating the centenary of Morgan's birth.

Which to include? Must have been an all but impossible task for Hamish Whyte, the editor, but I'm sure you'll enjoy his choice as much as I do.

Morgan was made Scotland's first Makar (or national poet) of modern times in 2004 at the age of 84. Just in time to write *the* poem to be read at the opening of the Scottish

Parliament in its new building that year. Taking his cue from 'the auld makars who tickled a Scottish king's ear with melody and ribaldry and frank advice', he dished out his own truth to the new Parliamentarians – who had 'not wholly the power, not yet wholly the power' – insisting that when this poem was read out much emphasis had to be given to the *not yet*. Measured, magisterial, this work will have cried out to be included here.

In 'Aberdeen Train', a moment's glimpse from the window of an intercity express inspires a lyric of merely eleven lines that's as vividly visually realised as a perfect Chinese landscape. Equally clear-eyed, all the more moving for the restraint of its stark documentary realism, 'Death in Duke Street' faces the harshest of facts with the deepest humanity.

Memorably it was said of Morgan that he was fuelled by 'the intrinsic optimism of curiosity'. In his poetry hope and realism are not at odds. There's no denial of misery, violence, pain, but they are never given the last word.

There is blistering anger in 'Glasgow Sonnet V' and 'The Flowers of Scotland'. But to enjoy his playful, deeply creative, always inventive twisting of language and sound, try saying aloud the dialogues 'Canedolia' (a brilliant play on Scottish place-names) or 'Itinerary'.

As well as profoundly serious, he was always great fun. I can still see him on his 89th birthday when he was brought over to the Scottish Poetry Library in Edinburgh for the opening of the Edwin Morgan Archive. Crisply elegant linen blazer, pale lemon yellow, under it a mock-Warhol, nod-to-Pop-Art T-shirt with a metallic gold, silver and red striped appliqué of an iconic Tunnock's Caramel Wafer. But when one looked closer, the name emblazoned there was Glasgow.

Edwin Morgan was indeed Glasgow's own. He doesn't belong to Glasgow though, but to all of Scotland in all times, to Europe, to the whole world, to poetry itself and, above all, to the transcendent, transforming power of imagination.

Liz Lochhead

SCOTLAND

ABERDEEN TRAIN

Rubbing a glistening circle
on the steamed-up window I framed
a pheasant in a field of mist.
The sun was a great red thing somewhere low,
struggling with the milky scene. In the furrows
a piece of glass winked into life,
hypnotized the silly dandy; we
hooted past him with his head cocked,
contemplating a bottle-end,
and this was the last of October,
a Chinese moment in the Mearns.

The Second Life
(Edinburgh University Press, 1968)

CANEDOLIA

an off-concrete Scotch fantasia

oa! hoy! awe! ba! mey!

who saw?
rhu saw rum. garve saw smoo. nigg saw tain. lairg saw lagg.
rig saw eigg. largs saw haggs. tongue saw luss. mull saw
yell. stoer saw strone. drem saw muck. gask saw noss. unst
saw cults. echt saw banff. weem saw wick. trool saw twatt.

how far?
from largo to lunga from joppa to skibo from ratho to
shona from ulva to minto from tinto to tolsta from soutra
to marsco from braco to barra from alva to stobo from
fogo to fada from gigha to gogo from kelso to stroma from
hirta to spango.

what is it like there?
och, it's freuchie, it's faifley, it's wamphray, it's frandy, it's
sliddery.

what do you do?
we foindle and fungle, we bonkle and meigle and
maxpoffle. we scotstarvit, armit, wormit, and even
whifflet. we play at crossstobs, leuchars, gorbals, and

finfan. we scavaig, and there's aye a bit of tilquhilly. if it's
wet, treshnish and mishnish.

what is the best of the country?
blinkbonny! airgold! thundergay!

and the worst?
scrishven, shiskine, scrabster, and snizort.

listen! what's that?
catacol and wauchope, never heed them.

tell us about last night
well, we had a wee ferintosh and we lay on the quiraing. it
was pure strontian!

but who was there?
petermoidart and craigenkenneth and cambusputtock and
ecclemuchty and corriehulish and balladolly and
altnacanny and clauchanvrechan and stronachlochan and
auchenlachar and tighnacrankie and tilliebruaich and
killieharra

and invervannach and achnatudlem and machrishellach
and inchtamurchan and auchterfechan and kinlochculter
and ardnawhallie and invershuggle.

and what was the toast?
schiehallion! schiehallion! schiehallion!

The Second Life
(Edinburgh University Press, 1968)

COLUMBA'S SONG

Where's Brude? Where's Brude?
So many souls to be saved!
The bracken is thick, the wildcat is quick,
the foxes dance in the moonlight,
the salmon dance in the waters,
the adders dance in the thick brown bracken.
Where's Brude? Where's man?
There's too much nature here,
eagles and deer,
but where's the mind, and where's the soul?
Show me your kings, your women, the man of the plough.
And cry me to your cradles.
It wasn't for a fox or an eagle I set sail!

Twelve Songs
(The Castlelaw Press, 1970)

THE CHAFFINCH MAP OF SCOTLAND

chaffinch
chaffinchchaffinch
chaffinchchaffinchchaffinch
chaffinchchaffinchchaffinch
chaffinchchaffinch
  chaffinch
chaffie chye chaffiechaffie
chaffie chye chaffiechaffie
      chye chaffie
      chaffiechaffiechaffie
      chaffiechaffiechaffie
        chaffiechaffie
        chaffiechaffie
        chaffiechaffie
        chaffiechaffie

          shilly shelly
          shelfyshilfyshellyshilly

shilfyshellyshelly
shilfyshelfyshelly
shellyfaw
shielyshellyfaw

shilfy
shilfyshefy shielyshiely   shielychaffie   chaffiechaffie
shilfyshelfyshelfy
chaffiechaffie
chaffiechaffie
shilfyshilfyshilfyshelfyshelfy
chaffieshilfyshilfyshelfyshelfyshelfyshelfy
chaffieshilfyshilfyshelfyshelfyshelfyshelfyshelfy
shilfyshilfyshilfyshelfy   shelfyshefy
shilfy   shilfy
shilfy
shilfyshelfy

brichtie

The Second Life
(Edinburgh University Press, 1968)

A CITY

– What was all that then? – What? – *That*. That was *Glasgow*.
It's a film, an epic, lasts for, anyway
keep watching, it's not real, so everything is
melting at the edges and could go, you have to
remember some of it was shot in Moscow,
parts in Chicago, and then of course the people
break up occasionally, they're only graphics,
look there's two businessmen gone zigzag, they'll be
off-screen in one moment, yes, I thought so.
– What a sky though. – Ah well, the sky is listed,
change as it may. It's a peculiar platinum
with roary sunset flecks and fissures, rigging
was best against it, gone now, don't regret it,
move on, and if you wait you'll see some children,
oh it's a fine effect, maybe they're real, some
giant children pulling down a curtain
of platinum and scarlet stuff as airy
as it seems strong, and they'll begin to play there,
bouncing their shrill cries till it's too dark to
catch a shadow running along the backcloth,
and they still won't go home, despite the credits.
– You mean the film goes on, beyond the credits?
– You'll have to wait and see, won't you? It's worth it.
– I'm not persuaded even of its existence.

– What, *Glasgow?* – The city, not the film. – The city
is the film. – Oh come on. – I tell you. – Right then,
look. Renfield Street, marchers, banners, slogans.
Read the message, hear the chant. – Lights! Camera!
– But where are the children? – That I grant you;
somewhere, huge presences; shouting, laughter;
hunch-cuddy-hunch against a phantom housewall.

Hold Hands among the Atoms
(Mariscat Press, 1991)

DEATH IN DUKE STREET

A huddle on the greasy street –
cars stop, nose past, withdraw –
dull glint on soles of tackety boots,
frayed rough trousers, nondescript coat
stretching back, head supported
in strangers' arms, a crowd collecting –
'Whit's wrang?' 'Can ye see'm?'
'An auld fella, he's had it.'
On one side, a young mother in a headscarf
is kneeling to comfort him, her three-year-old son
stands puzzled, touching her coat, her shopping-bag
spills its packages that people look at
as they look at everything. On the other side
a youth, nervous, awkwardly now
at the centre of attention as he shifts his arm
on the old man's shoulders, wondering
what to say to him, glancing up at the crowd.
These were next to him when he fell,
and must support him into death.
He seems not to be in pain,
he is speaking slowly and quietly
but he does not look at any of them,
his eyes are fixed on the sky,

already he is moving out
beyond everything belonging.
As if he still belonged
they hold him very tight.

Only the hungry ambulance
howls for him through the staring squares.

From Glasgow to Saturn
(Carcanet Press, 1973)

Yes, it is too cold in Scotland for flower people; in any case
who would be handed a thistle?
What are our flowers? Locked swings and private rivers –
and the island of Staffa for sale in the open market, which
no one questions or thinks strange –
and lads o' pairts that run to London and Buffalo without a
backward look while their elders say Who'd blame them –
and bonny fechters kneedeep in dead ducks with all the
thrawn intentness of the incorrigible professional Scot –
and a Kirk Assembly that excels itself in the bad old rhetoric
and tries to stamp out every glow of charity and change,
most wrong when it thinks most loudly it is most right –
and a Scottish National Party that refuses to discuss Vietnam
and is even applauded for doing so, do they think no lesson
is to be learned from what is going on there? –
and the unholy power of Grouse-moor and Broad-acres to
prevent the smoke of useful industry from sullying
Invergordon or setting up linear cities among the whaups –
and the banning of Beardsley and Joyce but not of course of
'Monster on the Campus' or 'Curse of the Undead' – those
who think the former are the more degrading, what are
their values? –
and the steady creep of the preservationist societies, wearing
their pens out for slums with good leaded lights – if they
could buy all the amber in the Baltic and melt it over

Edinburgh would they be happy then? – the skeleton is
    well-proportioned –
and by contrast the massive indifference to the slow death
    of the Clyde estuary, decline of resorts. loss of steamers,
    anaemia of yachting, cancer of monstrous installations
    of a foreign power and an acquiescent government –
    what is the smell of death on a child's spade, any more
    than rats to leaded lights? –
and dissidence crying in the wilderness to a moor of
    boulders and two ospreys –
these are the flowers of Scotland.

Penguin Modern Poets 15
(Penguin Books, 1969)

Open the doors! Light of the day, shine in; light of the mind,
    shine out!
We have a building which is more than a building.
There is a commerce between inner and outer, between
    brightness and shadow, between the world and those who
    think about the world.
Is it not a mystery? The parts cohere, they come together
    like petals of a flower, yet they also send their tongues
    outward to feel and taste the teeming earth.
Did you want classic columns and predictable pediments?
    A growl of old Gothic grandeur? A blissfully boring box?
Not here, no thanks! No icon, no IKEA, no iceberg, but
    curves and caverns, nooks and niches, huddles and
    heavens, syncopations and surprises. Leave symmetry
    to the cemetery.
But bring together slate and stainless steel, black granite
    and grey granite, seasoned oak and sycamore, concrete
    blond and smooth as silk – the mix is almost alive – it
    breathes and beckons – imperial marble it is not!

Come down the Mile, into the heart of the city, past the kirk
    of St Giles and the closes and wynds of the noted ghosts
    of history who drank their claret and fell down the steep
    tenement stairs into the arms of link-boys but who wrote

and talked the starry Enlightenment of their days –
And before them the auld makars who tickled a Scottish
    king's ear with melody and ribaldry and frank advice –
And when you are there, down there, in the midst of things,
    not set upon an hill with your nose in the air,
This is where you know your parliament should be
And this is where it is, just here.

What do the people want of the place? They want it to be
    filled with thinking persons as open and adventurous as
    its architecture.
A nest of fearties is what they do not want.
A symposium of procrastinators is what they do not want.
A phalanx of forelock-tuggers is what they do not want.
And perhaps above all the droopy mantra of 'it wizny me' is
    what they do not want.
Dear friends, dear lawgivers, dear parliamentarians, you
    are picking up a thread of pride and self-esteem that has
    been almost but not quite, oh no not quite, not ever
    broken or forgotten.

When you convene you will be reconvening, with a sense of
    not wholly the power, not yet wholly the power, but a
    good sense of what was once in the honour of your grasp.
All right. Forget, or don't forget, the past. Trumpets and
    robes are fine, but in the present and the future you will
    need something more.
What is it? We, the people, cannot tell you yet, but you will know
    about it when we do tell you.
We give you our consent to govern, don't pocket it and ride
    away.
We give you our deepest dearest wish to govern well, don't
    say we have no mandate to be so bold.
We give you this great building, don't let your work and
    hope be other than great when you enter and begin.
So now begin. Open the doors and begin.

A Book of Lives
(Carcanet Press, 2007)

GLASGOW SONNET V

'Let them eat cake' made no bones about it.
But we say let them eat the hope deferred
and that will sicken them. We have preferred
silent slipways to the riveters' wit.
And don't deny it – that's the ugly bit.
Ministers' tears might well have launched a herd
of bucking tankers if they'd been transferred
from Whitehall to the Clyde. And smiles don't fit
either. 'There'll be no bevvying' said Reid
at the work-in. But all the dignity you muster
can only give you back a mouth to feed
and rent to pay if what you lose in bluster
is no more than win patience with 'I need'
while distant blackboards use you as their duster.

Glasgow Sonnets
(The Castlelaw Press, 1972)

ITINERARY

I

We went to Oldshoremore.
Is the Oldshoremore road still there?
You mean the old shore road?
I suppose it's more an old road than a shore road.
No more! They shored it up, but it's washed away.
So you could sing the old song –
Yes we sang the old song:
    We'll take the old Oldshoremore shore road no more.

We passed the Muckle Flugga.
Did you see the muckle flag?
All we saw was the muckle fog.
The flag says ULTIMA FLUGGA WHA'S LIKE US.
Couldn't see flag for fug, sorry.
Ultimately –
    Ultimately we made for Muck and flogged the lugger.

III

Was it bleak at Bowhousebog?
It was black as a hoghouse, boy.
Yes, but bleak?
Look, it was black as a bog and bleak as the Bauhaus!
The Bauhaus wasn't black –
Will you get off my back!
So there were dogs too?
    Dogs, hogs, leaks in the bogs – we never went back.

From Glasgow to Saturn
(Carcanet Press, 1973)

THE LITTLE WHITE ROWS
OF SCOTLAND

whitewhitewhitewhitewhitewhitewhitewhitewhitemeigle
whitewhitewhitewhitewhitewhitewhitewhitemacadamwhite
whitewhitewhitewhitewhitewhitewhiterizziowhitewhite
whitewhitewhitewhitewhitewhitefaslanewhitewhitewhite
whitewhitewhitewhitewhitenapierwhitewhitewhitewhite
whitewhitewhitewhiteduntulmwhitewhitewhitewhitewhite
whitewhitewhiteyarrowwhitewhitewhitewhitewhitewhite
whitewhitecurlingwhitewhitewhitewhitewhitewhitewhite
whitemaxtonwhitewhitewhitewhitewhitewhitewhitewhite
allowaywhitewhitewhitewhitewhitewhitewhitewhitewhite

Poems of Thirty Years
(Carcanet Press, 1983)

[22]

QUESTIONS I

If mony a pickle maks a puckle
Does mony a mickle mak a muckle?
If we are aw Jock Tamson's bairns
Whit's the pynt o biggin cairns?
If yir face is trippin you
Zat mean it's really crippling you?
Let that flee stick tae the waw –
Wull it no come aff an aw?
Zeenty teenty tethery dumpty –
Kin ye no say wan two three, ya numpty?
If sumdy cries, Yir baw's on the slates,
Dae ye luk fur a ledder or pit oan yir skates?
If facts are chiels that winna ding
Dae dreams no go their dinger and sing?
They say a gaun fit is ay gettin:
D'ye think aik an yew stert sweatin?
Better a wee bush than nae bield:
Bare-scud Picts on the battlefield?
Speak o the Deil an he appears.
Speak o Gode – nae fears, nae fears!

A Book of Lives
(Carcanet Press, 2007)

[23]

ROCKALL INVERNESSSHIRE
JUNE 1972

A megagrampus in granite,
a snout surfacing for air and frozen for ever
in the blasts of the Atlantic,
the rock gets a ring in its muzzle,
it is man's.
But only just: for in this picture
a midnight gale too wild for work
even in the simmer-dim
has triggered off an eerie blink
from the unfinished beacon on the summit
and warns men before
men warn men.

Instamatic Poems
(Ian McKelvie, 1972)

from SONNETS FROM SCOTLAND

SLATE

There is no beginning. We saw Lewis
laid down, when there was not much but thunder
and volcanic fires; watched long seas plunder
faults; laughed as Staffa cooled. Drumlins blue as
bruises were grated off like nutmegs; bens,
and a great glen, gave a rough back we like
to think the ages must streak, surely strike,
seldom stroke, but raised and shaken, with tens
of thousands of rains, blizzards, sea-poundings
shouldered off into night amd memory.
Memory of men! That was to come. Great
in their empty hunger these surroundings
threw walls to the sky, the sorry glory
of a rainbow. Their heels kicked flint, chalk, slate.

THE PICTS

Names as from outer space, names without roots:
Bes, son of Nanammovvezz; Bliesblituth
that wild buffoon throned in an oaken booth;
wary Edarnon; brilliant Usconbuts;
Canutulachama who read the stars.
Where their fame flashed from, went to, is unknown.
The terror of their warriors is known,
naked, tattooed on every part (the hairs
of the groin are shaved on greatest fighters,
the fine bone needle dipped in dark-blue woad
rings the flesh with tender quick assurance:
he is *diuperr cartait*, rich pin; writers
like us regain mere pain on that blue road,
they think honour comes with the endurance).

MEMENTO

over the cliff-top and into the mist
across the heather and down to the peat
here with the sheep and where with the peeweet
through the stubble and by the pheasant's tryst
above the pines and past the northern lights
along the voe and out to meet the ice
among the stacks and round their kreidekreis
in summer lightning and beneath white nights
behind the haar and in front of the tower
beyond the moor and against writ and ring
below the mort-gate and outwith all kind
under the hill and at the boskless bower
over the hills and far away to bring
over the hills and far away to mind

THE AGE OF HERACLEUM

The jungle of Gleneagles was a long
shadow on our right as we travelled down.
Boars rummaged through the ballroom's toppled crown
of chandeliers and mashed the juicy throng
of giant hogweed stalks. Wild tramps with sticks
glared, kept a rough life. South in Fife we saw
the rusty buckled bridges, the firth raw
with filth and flower-heads, dead fish, dark slicks.
We stood in what had once been Princes Street.
Hogweed roots thrust, throbbed underneath for miles.
The rubble of the shops became the food
of new cracks running mazes round our feet,
and west winds blew, past shattered bricks and tiles,
millions of seeds through ruined Holyrood.

THE COIN

We brushed the dirt off, held it to the light.
The obverse showed us *Scotland*, and the head
of a red deer; the antler-glint had fled
but the fine cut could still be felt. All right:
we turned it over, read easily *One Pound*,
but then the shock of Latin, like a gloss,
Respublica Scotorum, sent across
such ages as we guessed but never found
at the worn edge where once the date had been
and where as many fingers had gripped hard
as hopes their silent race had lost or gained.
The marshy scurf crept up to our machine,
sucked at our boots. Yet nothing seemed ill-starred.
And least of all the realm the coin contained.

THE SOLWAY CANAL

Slowly through the Cheviot hills at dawn
we sailed. The high steel bridge at Carter Bar
passed over us in fog with not a car
in its broad lanes. Our hydrofoil slid on,
vibrating quietly through wet rock walls
and scarves of dim half-sparkling April mist;
a wizard with a falcon on his wrist
was stencilled on our bow. Rough waterfalls
flashed on that northern island of the Scots
as the sun steadily came up and cast
red light along the uplands and the waves,
and gulls with open beaks tore out our thoughts
through the thick glass to where the Eildons massed,
or down to the Canal's drowned borderers' graves.

A GOLDEN AGE

That must have been a time of happiness.
The air was mild, the Campsie Fells had vines.
Dirigible parties left soft sky-signs
and bursts of fading music. Who could guess
what they might not accomplish, they had seas
in cities, cities in the sea; their domes
and crowded belvederes hung free, their homes
eagle-high or down among whitewashed quays.
And women sauntered often with linked arms
through night streets, or alone, or danced a maze
with friends. Perhaps it did not last. What lasts?
The bougainvillea millenniums
may come and go, but then in thistle days
a strengthened seed outlives the hardest blasts.

Sonnets from Scotland
(Mariscat Press, 1984)

ABOUT THE AUTHOR

EDWIN MORGAN (1920–2010) was born in Glasgow, and spent his life there except for his six years with the Royal Army Medical Corps in the Middle East. He studied English Literature at the University of Glasgow, where he went on to teach, retiring as Professor Emeritus in 1980. He was appointed Glasgow's Poet Laureate in 1999, and awarded the Queen's Gold Medal for Poetry in 2000. In 2004 he was appointed the first Scots Makar of modern times, and wrote the poem 'For the Opening of the Scottish Parliament' in the same year. His poetry is praised for its linguistic inventiveness, social realism and humane curiosity. He wrote concrete and visual poetry, opera libretti and collaborated with jazz saxophonist Tommy Smith to set his work to music; he was also a translator, playwright and critic. Morgan's work is renowned for its outward-looking internationalism, his poetic gaze moving from Europe to the wider world and into space, yet always returning to Glasgow, whose people and landscape he so memorably evoked and imagined.